$\mathcal{A}$DVENT *and* $\mathcal{C}$HRISTMAS $\mathcal{W}$ISDOM

—— *from* ——

POPE JOHN PAUL II

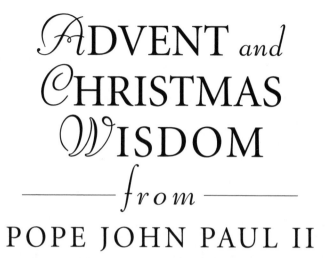

Advent and Christmas Wisdom from

POPE JOHN PAUL II

Daily Scripture and Prayers
Together With
Pope John Paul II's Own Words

Compiled by John V. Kruse, PhD

Liguori
LIGUORI, MISSOURI

Imprimi Potest:
Thomas D. Picton, C.Ss.R.
Provincial, Denver Province
The Redemptorists

Published by Liguori Publications
Liguori, Missouri
www.liguori.org

Library of Congress Cataloging-in-Publication Data

John Paul II, 1920–2005.
    Advent and Christmas wisdom from Pope John Paul II : daily scripture and prayers together with Pope John Paul II's own words / compiled by John V. Kruse.—1st ed.
       p. cm.
    Includes bibliographical references.
    ISBN-13: 978-0-7648-1510-2 ; ISBN-10: 0-7648-1510-5 (alk. paper)
    1. Advent—Prayer-books and devotions—English. 2. Christmas—Prayer-books and devotions—English. 3. Catholic Church—Prayer-books and devotions—English. I. Kruse, John V. II. Title.
BX2170.A4J64 2006
242'.33—dc22
                                                2006018685

Printed in the United States of America
10 09 08 07 06   5 4 3 2 1
First edition

Contents

Epigraph

TODAY THE SEASON OF ADVENT BEGINS, the journey of spiritual renewal in preparation for Christmas. The voices of the prophets who proclaim the Messiah ring out in the liturgy asking for conversion of heart and for prayer. John the Baptist, the last of these and the greatest, cries out: *Prepare the way of the Lord!* (Luke 3:4), because he *will come to visit his people in peace.*

Come Christ, Prince of Peace! Preparing for his birth means reawakening the hope of peace in ourselves and throughout the world. Build peace in hearts first of all, by laying down the weapons of rancor, revenge, and every form of selfishness.

POPE JOHN PAUL II, ANGELUS, NOVEMBER 30, 2003

Introduction

FROM EARLY IN HIS PONTIFICATE, it became clear that Pope John Paul II desired to lead the Church into the third millennium. During the millennial celebration, he sought to instill a fuller appreciation of the significance of the Incarnation, a cause of great hope and rejoicing for all of humankind. He called all the faithful to a deeper and renewed relationship with Christ. In addition, he sought to make the jubilee year one of healing, forgiveness, and reconciliation in the world. As expressed in his apostolic letter, *Novo millennio ineunte*, a central theme for the jubilee celebration of the new millennium was Hebrews 13:8—*Jesus Christ is the same yesterday and today and forever.* In fact, the Latin *Christus heri, hodie, semper,* or "Christ yesterday, today, forever," appeared on the official logo for the millennial jubilee. This threefold theme of the advent of the new millennium summarizes our encounter with Christ in every Advent season. We remember Christ's Incarnation over two thousand years ago. We yearn for and welcome Christ's presence in our lives today. We look forward to the future coming of Christ in glory. Through his prophetic words and inspiring example, Pope John Paul II courageously led the Church into the third millennium. May he similarly guide us in our encounter with Christ this Advent and Christmas.

HOW TO USE THIS BOOK

Advent—that period of great anticipatory joy—is a time of preparation for the celebration of Jesus' arrival in Bethlehem as a helpless infant. In the Western liturgy, Advent begins four Sundays prior to December 25—the Sunday closest to November 30, which is the feast of Saint Andrew, Jesus' first disciple. The annual commemoration of Jesus' birth begins the Christmas cycle of the liturgical year—a cycle that runs from Christmas Eve to the Sunday after the feast of the Epiphany. In keeping with the unfolding of the message of the liturgical year, this book is designed to be used during the entire period from the First Sunday of Advent to the end of the Christmas cycle. The four weeks of Advent are often thought of as symbolizing the four different ways that Jesus comes into the world: (1) at his birth as a helpless infant at Bethlehem; (2) at his arrival in the hearts of believers; (3) at his death; and (4) at his arrival on Judgment Day.

Because Christmas falls on a different day of the week each year, the fourth week of Advent is never really finished; it is abruptly, joyously, and solemnly abrogated by the annual coming again of Jesus at Christmas. Christ's Second Coming will also one day abruptly interrupt our sojourn here on earth.

Since the calendar dictates the number of days in Advent, this book includes Scripture and meditation readings for a full twenty-eight days. These twenty-eight daily readings make up part I of this book. It is suggested that the reader begin at the beginning and, on Christmas, switch to part II, which contains materials for the twelve days of Christmas. If there are any "extra" entries from part I, these may be read by doubling up days, if so desired, or by reading two entries on weekends. Alternately, one may just skip these entries that do not fit within the Advent time frame for that particular year.

Part III of this book proposes two optional formats for using each daily entry as part of a longer liturgical observance similar to Night Prayer combined with a version of the Office of Readings. These options are for those who may wish to use this book as part of a more-developed individual or group observance. The purpose of these readings is to enrich the Advent/Christmas/Epiphany season of the liturgical year and set up a means by which individuals, families, or groups may observe the true meaning of the season.

PART I

~~~~~~

READINGS *for* ADVENT

DAY 1

Entering the Season, Contemplating the Mystery

*D*earest Brothers and Sisters[:] With today's first Sunday of Advent, a new liturgical year begins. The Church takes up her journey again, and invites us to reflect more intensely on the mystery of Christ, a mystery that is always new and that time cannot exhaust. Christ is the Alpha and the Omega, the beginning and the end. Thanks to him, the history of humanity proceeds as a pilgrimage toward the fulfillment of the Kingdom which he inaugurated with his Incarnation and victory over sin and death.

JOHN PAUL II, ANGELUS, DECEMBER 2, 2001

The Depth of God's Love Revealed

Blessed be the God and Father of our Lord Jesus Christ, who has blessed us in Christ with every spiritual blessing in the heavenly places, just as he chose us in Christ before the foundation of the world to be holy and blameless before him in love. He destined us for adoption as his children through Jesus Christ, according to the good pleasure of his will, to the praise of his glorious grace that he freely bestowed on us in the Beloved. In him we have redemption through his blood, the forgiveness of our trespasses, according to the riches of his grace that he lavished on us. With all wisdom and insight he has made known to us the mystery of his will, according to his good pleasure that he set forth in Christ, as a plan for the fullness of time, to gather up all things in him, things in heaven and things on earth.

EPHESIANS 1:3–10

Prayer

Loving God, source of my ultimate longing, you have reached out to your people through the gift of your incarnate Son. Today in a special way I start anew my spiritual journey toward the stable where I seek to encounter the babe of Bethlehem. Be with me, guide me, teach me, strengthen me, and inspire me during this journey. Draw me into closer union with you as I put forth my best effort to prepare for the coming of Christ so that I may truly present him with a gift worth giving on Christmas day.

Advent Action

What is it specifically that you hope to achieve this Advent season? Take the time to give this question serious thought. Write down a few thoughts on a piece of paper. Keep this paper in this book and refer to it regularly as you engage in your daily meditations.

Prepare the Way of the Lord

*I*n…[the Gospel of Luke] the figure of John the Baptist appears, the prophet sent to prepare the way for the Messiah. His voice cries out "in the wilderness" where he had withdrawn and where, as the Evangelist Luke says, "the word of God came to [him]" (Luke 3:2).

John the Baptist's cry reechoes from generation to generation: "Prepare the way of the Lord, make his paths straight. Every valley shall be filled, and every mountain and hill shall be brought low, and the crooked shall be made straight, and the rough ways shall be made smooth" (Luke 3:4–5). How urgent and timely is this call at both the personal and social level! God wants to come and dwell with the people of every time and place, and he calls them to cooperate with him in the work of salvation.

But how?…[Luke's Gospel] gives us the answer: we must "straighten" injustices, "fill" the void with goodness, mercy, respect and understanding, "bring low" pride, barriers and violence, and "make smooth" all that prevents people from living a free and dignified life. Only in this way can we prepare to celebrate Christmas in an authentic way.

JOHN PAUL II, ANGELUS, DECEMBER 7, 1997

CALL FOR JUSTICE

> *Wash yourselves; make yourselves clean;*
>> *remove the evil of your doings*
>> *from before my eyes;*
> *cease to do evil,*
>> *learn to do good;*
> *seek justice,*
>> *rescue the oppressed,*
> *defend the orphan,*
>> *plead for the widow.*

ISAIAH 1:16–17

PRAYER

Lord, help me to prepare for your coming. You call me to right injustices…in my own life, in my local community, in my nation, and in the world. Help me to be prepared for your coming by giving me the strength and courage to fight injustice wherever I encounter it.

ADVENT ACTION

What injustices do you see around you in the world? Obviously, you cannot correct every injustice, but what steps (even small ones) can you take today to "make the crooked straight"? Make a commitment today to join and/or financially support an organization that promotes greater justice.

DAY 3

Waiting With Patience

*A*dvent invites us to rejoice, and at the same time, it exhorts us to wait with patience for the coming of the Lord now approaching. It exhorts us not to be discouraged, to resist every kind of adversity, with the certainty that the Lord will not delay his coming.

This vigilant patience...favors the strengthening of human ties in the Christian community. The faithful realize that they are little ones who are poor and in great need of God's help, and they come together to receive the Messiah who is about to come. He will come in the silence, the humility, the poverty of the crib, and will bring his joy to all who welcome him with open hearts.

JOHN PAUL II, HOMILY, PASTORAL VISIT TO THE ROMAN PARISH OF ST. MARÍA JOSEFA OF THE HEART OF JESUS, DECEMBER 16, 2001

TRUSTING THAT HE IS NEAR

Be patient, therefore, beloved, until the coming of the Lord. The farmer waits for the precious crop from the earth, being patient with it until it receives the early and the late rains. You also must be patient. Strengthen your hearts, for the coming of the Lord is near.

JAMES 5:7–8
[THIS PASSAGE SERVES AS THE THEME OF JOHN PAUL II'S HOMILY.]

PRAYER

Jesus, Lord of our longings, it seems that patience is a lost virtue in the modern world. We expect instant results and gratification. Often, when we wait, we feel as if we are wasting time. In reality, waiting often deepens our sense of appreciation for that which we await. Teach me the virtue of patience. Help me to see that waiting only makes me appreciate even more the gift of your coming. Truly, good things do come to those who wait.

ADVENT ACTION

When circumstances cause you to wait today (for example, traffic delays, in line at a store, or while waiting to pick up a child at sports practice), try to do so with patience. Turn your waiting into an opportunity. Use the time for prayer and to reach a deeper recognition of your own longing for the coming of the Lord into your life.

DAY 4

The Incarnation: Source of Answers to Life's Ultimate Questions

*A*ncient history shows clearly how in different parts of the world, with their different cultures, there arise at the same time the fundamental questions which pervade human life: *Who am I? Where have I come from and where am I going? Why is there evil? What is there after this life?*...These are questions which have their common source in the quest for meaning which has always compelled the human heart. In fact, the answer given to these questions decides the direction which people seek to give to their lives.

The Church is no stranger to this journey of discovery, nor could she ever be. From the moment when, through the Paschal Mystery, she received the gift of the ultimate truth about human life, the Church has made her pilgrim way along the paths of the world to proclaim that Jesus Christ is "the way, and the truth, and the life" (John 14:6).

JOHN PAUL II, *FIDES ET RATIO*
(FAITH AND REASON), 1–2, SEPTEMBER 14, 1998

LOOKING TO CHRIST FOR ANSWERS

So Jesus asked the twelve, "Do you also wish to go away?" Simon Peter answered him, "Lord, to whom can we go? You have the words of eternal life. We have come to believe and know that you are the Holy One of God."

JOHN 6:67–69

PRAYER

Lord, there are many things in life that I don't understand. There are many questions that I have. Yet I know that you have taken on human flesh in order to show me the way to find meaning in life and to lead me to the answers that I seek. May the questions that I have lead me to a deeper union with you, the source of all truth.

ADVENT ACTION

What questions do you have for God? Have you been waiting on God for answers? Are you open to hearing God's answers? Reflect on how the fact that God became human for your salvation might provide answers to your questions. Remember that we can begin to find the answers to the tough questions of life in the word of God. Spend a few extra minutes reading one of your favorite Scripture passages or perhaps the *Lectionary* readings for the day, which should be indicated in your church bulletin.

DAY 5

God Seeks Us

In Jesus Christ God not only speaks to man but also *seeks him out.* The Incarnation of the Son of God attests that God goes in search of man. Jesus speaks of this search as the finding of a lost sheep (see Luke 15:1–7). It is a search which *begins in the heart of God* and culminates in the Incarnation of the Word. If God goes in search of man, created in his own image and likeness, he does so because he loves him eternally in the Word, and wishes to raise him in Christ to the dignity of an adoptive son. God therefore goes in search of man who *is his special possession* in a way unlike any other creature. Man is God's possession by virtue of a choice made in love: God seeks man out, moved by his fatherly heart.

JOHN PAUL II, *TERTIO MILLENNIO ADVENIENTE*
(AS THE THIRD MILLENNIUM DRAWS NEAR), 7, NOVEMBER 10, 1994

God's Longing to Find Us

"Or what woman having ten silver coins, if she loses one of them, does not light a lamp, sweep the house, and search carefully until she finds it? When she has found it, she calls together her friends and neighbors, saying, 'Rejoice with me, for I have found the coin that I had lost.' Just so, I tell you, there is joy in the presence of the angels of God over one sinner who repents."

LUKE 15:8–10

Prayer

God, I often feel lost in this world. There are many messages bombarding me, telling me which way to go. In my restlessness, I know that I long for something more than what this world has to offer. Thankfully, I do not have to find my way through all these conflicting messages on my own. Out of your great love for me, you have sent your Son to find me amid the confusion of this world. I pray in a special way today that Jesus will take me by the hand and lead me to a life beyond anything what the world has to offer: life in you.

Advent Action

What barriers in your life are you erecting to prevent God from finding you this Advent season? Are you keeping too busy? Are you caught up in the materialism of the season? Are you burdened by worry and anxiety? Is there some activity in which you are involved that is keeping a distance between you and God? Tear down at least one barrier that you have put up between yourself and God.

DAY 6

Making Our Families Holy and Whole

*F*amily communion can only be preserved and perfected through a great spirit of sacrifice. It requires, in fact, a ready and generous openness of each and all to understanding, to forbearance, to pardon, to reconciliation. There is no family that does not know how selfishness, discord, tension and conflict violently attack and at times mortally wound its own communion: hence there arise the many and varied forms of division in family life. But, at the same time, every family is called by the God of peace to have the joyous and renewing experience of "reconciliation," that is, communion reestablished, unity restored. In particular, participation in the sacrament of Reconciliation and in the banquet of the one Body of Christ offers to the Christian family the grace and the responsibility of overcoming every division and of moving towards the fullness of communion.

JOHN PAUL II, *FAMILIARIS CONSORTIO* (ON THE CHRISTIAN FAMILY IN THE MODERN WORLD), 21, NOVEMBER 21, 1981

RECONCILING BEFORE APPROACHING THE LORD

So when you are offering your gift at the altar, if you remember that your brother or sister has something against you, leave your gift there before the altar and go; first be reconciled to your brother or sister, and then come and offer your gift.

MATTHEW 5:23–24

PRAYER

My brother Jesus, frequently there is much tension in families, including my own. Often, small arguments transform into major disputes that tear my family apart. We are prone to hold onto grudges. This is especially the case during Advent when stress levels are running high because of pressures coming at us from all different directions. Yet you remind us that as we prepare for your coming, it is most important that we make peace within our families. Grant us the wisdom to recognize our own shortcomings, the courage to admit that we are wrong, and the love needed to forgive others.

ADVENT ACTION

Take a moment to evaluate the health of the relationships in your own family. Are you holding on to any grudges? Do you need to ask for forgiveness from anyone? Do you need to forgive anyone? Having reflected, take whatever step is necessary to be an agent of reconciliation in your family so that you may offer your own gift to the Christ child with a clean heart.

DAY 7

Mary's Openness

*D*uring…Advent, the Liturgy puts particular emphasis on the figure of Mary. The beginning of the Incarnation of the Redeemer took place *in her heart,* from her *"Here I am"* full of faith, in reply to the divine call. If we wish to understand the genuine meaning of Christmas, *we must look at her,* call upon her.

Mary, Mother *par excellence,* helps us to understand the key words of the mystery of the birth of her divine Son: *humility, silence, wonder, joy.*

She exhorts us, first of all, to humility, so that God can find space in our heart, not darkened by pride and arrogance. She points out to us the value of *silence,* which knows how to listen to the song of the Angels and the crying of the Child, not stifling them by noise and confusion. Together with her, we stop before the Nativity scene with intimate *wonder,* savoring the simple and pure *joy* that this Child gives to humanity.

JOHN PAUL II, ANGELUS, DECEMBER 21, 2003

Mary's Song of Confidence

And Mary said,
"My soul magnifies the Lord,
and my spirit rejoices in God my Savior,
for he has looked with favor on the lowliness of his servant.
Surely, from now on all generations will call me blessed;
for the Mighty One has done great things for me,
and holy is his name.
His mercy is for those who fear him from generation
to generation.
He has shown strength with his arm;
he has scattered the proud in the thoughts
of their hearts.
He has brought down the powerful from their thrones,
and lifted up the lowly;
he has filled the hungry with good things,
and sent the rich away empty.
He has helped his servant Israel,
in remembrance of his mercy,
according to the promise he made to our ancestors,
to Abraham and to his descendants forever."

LUKE 1:46–55

Prayer

Mary, you are the model of faithfulness. As a young woman, you confidently opened yourself to God's will and became the mother of our Savior. You remained a faithful disciple of your Son throughout his life. During this Advent season, teach me to be humble so that I too might be open to God's will. Inspire me so that during the rest of my life I might follow your Son as faithfully as you did…to the foot of the cross.

ADVENT ACTION

Reflect on Mary's great faith and consider areas in your own life where you need to trust God more. Entrust those areas to God today. Pray the joyful mysteries of the rosary or even a single decade of the rosary.

Approaching the Mystery
of the Incarnation Through
Prayer and Contemplation

*W*e cannot come to the fullness of contemplation of the Lord's face by our own efforts alone, but by allowing grace to take us by the hand. Only *the experience of silence and prayer* offers the proper setting for the growth and development of a true, faithful and consistent knowledge of that mystery which finds its culminating expression in the solemn proclamation by the Evangelist Saint John: "And the Word became flesh and dwelt among us, full of grace and truth; we have beheld his glory, glory as of the only Son from the Father" (1:14).

JOHN PAUL II, *TERTIO MILLENNIO ADVENIENTE*
(AS THE THIRD MILLENNIUM DRAWS NEAR), 20, NOVEMBER 10, 1994

THE NEED FOR PRAYER AND REFLECTION

That evening, at sundown, they brought to him all who were sick or possessed with demons. And the whole city was gathered around the door. And he cured many who were sick with various diseases, and cast out many demons; and he would not permit the demons to speak, because they knew him. In the morning, while it was still very dark, he got up and went out to a deserted place, and there he prayed.

MARK 1:32–35

PRAYER

Word made flesh, during this Advent season it is impossible for me to grasp the full meaning of your Incarnation. What a wonder it is that the transcendent God has become one of us in order to share his divine life with us. I can only begin to grasp the depths of this mystery by withdrawing from the busyness of my daily life, placing myself before you in prayer, and allowing you to speak to me. As I do so now, Lord, help me to better appreciate and understand the real beauty and incomprehensible love demonstrated by your assumption of our humanity.

ADVENT ACTION

Take an additional ten minutes of quiet just to open yourself to God's word and to contemplate what it means to you that God became human. Do not rack your brain to unravel this mystery. Rather, open yourself to God's grace and let God speak to you.

DAY 9

Returning to the Lord During Advent

*T*his call by the Apostle [1 Corinthians 11:28] indicates at least indirectly the close link between the Eucharist and Penance. Indeed, if the first word of Christ's teaching, the first phrase of the Gospel Good News, was "Repent, and believe in the gospel" (*metanoeite*) (Mark 1:15) the Sacrament of the Passion, Cross and Resurrection seems to strengthen and consolidate in an altogether special way this call in our souls. The Eucharist and Penance thus become in a sense two closely connected dimensions of authentic life in accordance with the spirit of the Gospel, of truly Christian life. The Christ who calls to the Eucharistic banquet is always the same Christ who exhorts us to penance and repeats his "Repent" (Mark 1:15)....

...[I]t is certain that the Church of the new Advent, the Church that is continually preparing for the new coming of the Lord, must be the Church of the Eucharist and of Penance. Only when viewed in this spiritual aspect of her life and activity is she seen to be the Church of the divine mission, the Church *in statu missionis* [in the state of mission], as the Second Vatican Council has shown her to be.

JOHN PAUL II, *REDEMPTOR HOMINIS*
(THE REDEEMER OF MAN), 20, MARCH 4, 1978

PETER'S CALL TO REPENTANCE

Repent therefore, and turn to God so that your sins may be wiped out, so that times of refreshing may come from the presence of the Lord, and that he may send the Messiah appointed for you, that is, Jesus, who must remain in heaven until the time of universal restoration that God announced long ago through his holy prophets.

ACTS 3:19–21

PRAYER

Lord of second chances, Advent is a time not only of waiting but also of repentance and turning back to you. I want to be ready to receive you when you come, especially as I encounter you in the Eucharist. Advent is a season for me to get my life in order. Give me the strength to turn from those things in my life that keep me from you and help me to draw closer to you. In the words of the Psalm 51:10, "Create in me a clean heart, O God, and put a new and right spirit within me."

ADVENT ACTION

Make a special effort to celebrate your personal conversion this Advent through the sacrament of reconciliation. If possible, take part in a communal celebration of the sacrament in your parish. Such celebrations can be powerful experiences not only of our shared human weaknesses but also of the strength we can gather from one another as we repent and prepare for the Lord's coming.

DAY 10

Be Not Afraid

Fear not, I will help you" (Isaiah 41:13). God's promise, echoed by the Prophet, was entirely fulfilled in the *birth of Jesus in Bethlehem*. In him, God became one of us! For this reason, we need not fear; the season we are living of Advent *encourages us to hope*.

JOHN PAUL II, HOMILY, ADVENT MASS FOR THE STUDENTS
OF THE ROMAN STATE UNIVERSITIES, DECEMBER 11, 2003

But when the disciples saw him walking on the sea, they were terrified, saying, "It is a ghost!" And they cried out in fear. But immediately Jesus spoke to them and said, "Take heart, it is I; do not be afraid."

Peter answered him, "Lord, if it is you, command me to come to you on the water." He said, "Come." So Peter got out of the boat, started walking on the water, and came toward Jesus. But when he noticed the strong wind, he became frightened, and beginning to sink, he cried out, "Lord, save me!" Jesus immediately reached out his hand and caught him, saying to him, "You of little faith, why did you doubt?" When they got into the boat, the wind ceased. And those in the boat worshiped him, saying, "Truly you are the Son of God."

MATTHEW 14:26–33

PRAYER

Lord who calmed the stormy seas, no life is free of difficulties and worries. Mine is no different. But Advent is a season of comfort and assurance. I patiently await your coming into my own life in an ever-deeper way this Christmas. This gives me cause for great strength and comfort as I face the fears of my life. Come, Lord Jesus, calm my fears and teach me to trust in you.

ADVENT ACTION

Identify what it is that you most fear. In what areas of your life do you feel as if you are walking on water, just about to sink? Turn those issues or areas of your life over to the coming Christ child today. Make a special effort to be an encouraging and calming voice to those with whom you live and work.

DAY 11

The Evergreen: Symbol of Eternal Life

*N*ext to the crib, as in St Peter's Square, we find the traditional *"Christmas tree."* This too is an ancient tradition that exalts the value of life, for in the winter season *the evergreen fir* becomes a sign of *undying life. Christmas gifts* are usually placed on the tree or arranged at its base. The symbol thus also becomes eloquent in a typically Christian sense: it calls to mind the *"tree of life"* (see Genesis 2:9), a figure of Christ, God's supreme gift to humanity.

The message of the Christmas tree is consequently that *life stays "evergreen" if we make a gift of it:* not so much of material things, but of life itself: in friendship and sincere affection, in fraternal help and forgiveness, in time shared and reciprocal listening.

JOHN PAUL II, ANGELUS, DECEMBER 19, 2004

No Greater Love

"This is my commandment, that you love one another as I have loved you. No one has greater love than this, to lay down one's life for one's friends. You are my friends if you do what I command you."

JOHN 15:12–14

Prayer

Lord, you have taught me that I can find my life by losing it (see Mark 8:35). If I want to share eternal life with you, I need to lay my life down for others in the same manner that you laid down your life for all of humankind. May I recognize the true meaning of this season by making a gift of myself to others in the same way that you have given yourself as a gift to me.

Advent Action

Make a date with a friend today. Enjoy the reciprocal giving and taking of friendship. If the opportunity presents itself, play the part of a "secret Santa" by delivering a small, unexpected gift anonymously to a friend or relative.

DAY 12

Crib vs. Consumerism

*T*he most thought-provoking reminder of the Lord's birth, about to take place, comes from the Nativity scene which has already been set up in many homes.

The simplicity of the Crib, however, is in strong contrast to that concept of Christmas which advertisements present insistently. Even the beautiful tradition of exchanging Christmas gifts between relatives and friends is under the influence of consumerism, which risks obscuring the true meaning of Christ's birth. Indeed, this tradition of exchanging gifts is to be understood in the perspective of God's gift to humanity in the person of Jesus, of which our gifts in this celebration are a reflection and expression. It is all the more important, for this reason, to favor actions that manifest solidarity and openness toward the poor and needy.

Looking at the Crib, our gaze is especially fixed on the Virgin and on Joseph, who await the birth of Jesus.... [In them], we see realized the indispensable conditions to prepare ourselves for Jesus' birth. In the first place, interior silence and prayer, which allow one to contemplate the mystery that is commemorated. In the second place, the willingness to accept the will of God, in whatever way it is manifested.

JOHN PAUL II, ANGELUS, DECEMBER 22, 2002

GOD'S GIFT

…God, who is rich in mercy, out of the great love with which he loved us even when we were dead through our trespasses, made us alive together with Christ—by grace you have been saved—and raised us up with him and seated us with him in the heavenly places in Christ Jesus, so that in the ages to come he might show the immeasurable riches of his grace in kindness toward us in Christ Jesus.

EPHESIANS 2:4–7

PRAYER

Lord Jesus, when I contemplate a Nativity scene, I am reminded of your humble entry into our world. You show me that fulfillment in life is not to be found in material goods. This Advent and Christmas, help me to keep my focus on you rather than being distracted by the consumerism that surrounds the season. Be my strength as I strive to be as open to doing God's will as your mother and foster father were.

ADVENT ACTION

If you have not already done so, set up a Nativity scene in your home today. Let the Nativity scene remind you of the real meaning of Christmas: the gift of God's great love for us. Consider how you might avoid excessive consumerism this Christmas and, when possible, give the gift of yourself (that is, your time and love) rather than buying into the consumer mentality.

DAY 13

The Name "Jesus"

*J*esus! This name, by which Christ was known in his family and among his friends in Nazareth, exalted by the crowds and invoked by the sick during the years of his public ministry, calls to mind his identity and mission as Savior. In fact "Jesus" means "God saves." This name, in the supreme sacrifice of Golgotha, shone forth as a life-giving name in which God offers the grace of reconciliation and peace to all mankind.

In this name the Church finds her whole good, she invokes it unceasingly, she proclaims it with ever new ardor....It is the divine name which alone brings salvation "for there is no other name under heaven given among men by which we must be saved" (Acts 4:12). Jesus himself shows us the saving power of his name, giving us this consoling certitude: "If you ask anything of the Father, he will give it to you in my name" (John 16:23).

JOHN PAUL II, ANGELUS, DECEMBER 22, 1996

HONORING THE NAME OF JESUS

Let the same mind be in you that was in Christ Jesus,
who, though he was in the form of God,
did not regard equality with God
as something to be exploited,
but emptied himself,
taking the form of a slave,
being born in human likeness.
And being found in human form,
he humbled himself
and became obedient to the point of death—
even death on a cross.
Therefore God also highly exalted him
and gave him the name
that is above every name,
so that at the name of Jesus
every knee should bend,
in heaven and on earth and under the earth,
and every tongue should confess
that Jesus Christ is Lord,
to the glory of God the Father.

PHILIPPIANS 2:5–11

PRAYER

Names carry great significance. Jesus, your name tells me that you are my Savior. You have come into the world to rescue me from my own self-destructiveness and selfishness and to show me the path to life. During your own life, you instructed me to trust in the power of your name. Help me always to show proper respect for your name. I call on your name today and always. I am confident that you will place my needs before the Father in your name that my needs will be met.

ADVENT ACTION

Find a quiet place to meditate on the name of Jesus. Repeat the name numerous times to yourself. What feelings does the name evoke for you? Do you show respect for the name of Jesus in your own life? Make a concerted effort not to use Jesus' name in vain in the future. When you face a difficulty or challenge today, call upon the name of Jesus. During the remainder of the Advent season, remember the blessings and power associated with this name.

DAY 14

Joseph: Model of Faith, Justice, and Prayer

*M*atthew highlights the role of *Joseph* whom he describes as a "just" man (Matthew 1:19), and thus emphasizes his unreserved devotion to fulfilling God's will. Precisely because of this inner righteousness, which in the ultimate analysis *coincides with love*, Joseph does not decide to reject Mary when he discovers she is with child. He resolves to "send her away quietly" (Matthew 1:19), but the angel of the Lord tells him not to fear, and to take her as his wife.

Another essential aspect of Saint Joseph's personality emerges here: he is *ready to listen to God in prayer*. He learns from the angel that "it is through the Holy Spirit that this child has been conceived in her [Mary]" (see Matthew 1:20), according to the ancient prophecy: "*Behold, a young woman shall conceive…*," and he is quick to accept God's plans that surpass human limitations.

In sum, Joseph can be described as an authentic man of faith like his wife Mary. *Faith combines justice and prayer;* this is the most appropriate attitude with which to encounter the Emmanuel,

God-with-us. Indeed, believing means *living through history open to God's initiative,* to the creative force of his Word who became flesh in Christ, uniting himself to our humanity forever.

JOHN PAUL II, ANGELUS, DECEMBER 16, 2001

PLEASING GOD

> *To do righteousness and justice
> is more acceptable to the LORD than sacrifice.*

PROVERBS 21:3

PRAYER

Lord, I long to be like your faith-filled servant, Joseph. Help me to be open to your word in whatever form it may come to me. Inspired by him, may I come to trust in you as he did. After his example, may I treat all whom I encounter with justice.

ADVENT ACTION

God speaks to us in many different ways. God spoke to Joseph through dreams. Sometimes God speaks to us through events in our lives and those around us, perhaps even strangers or people whom we may not particularly like. Take a moment to consider how God may be speaking to you, especially in ways you may not have been open to previously.

Joseph was a righteous man who treated Mary with justice and compassion. Is there anyone in your life whom you are not treating with justice and compassion? Is there a family member, coworker, friend, or someone you pass on the street or in your office that you may be in the habit of overlooking? Make a point today to acknowledge the contribution he or she makes to your life. Treat all whom you encounter with justice.

DAY 15

Solidarity With the Marginalized

*T*he season of Advent…spurs us to prepare ourselves to welcome the Lord who will come [again in glory]. But how should we prepare? This important celebration we are holding highlights the fact that a concrete way to prepare ourselves for this meeting is by *closeness and sharing with those who, for whatever reason, are in difficulty.* By recognizing Christ in our brethren, we are preparing to be recognized by him at his final return. This is how the *Christian community prepares for the Lord's second coming:* by focusing on those persons whom Jesus himself favored, those who are often excluded and ignored by society

JOHN PAUL II, HOMILY, JUBILEE OF THE DISABLED, DECEMBER 3, 2000

THE FINAL JUDGMENT

"Then the king will say to those at his right hand, 'Come, you that are blessed by my Father, inherit the kingdom prepared for you from the foundation of the world; for I was hungry and you gave me food, I was thirsty and you gave me something to drink, I was a stranger and you welcomed me, I was naked and you gave me clothing, I was sick and you took care of me, I was in prison and you visited me.' Then the righteous will answer him, 'Lord, when was it that we saw you hungry and gave you food, or thirsty and gave you something to drink? And when was it that we saw you a stranger and welcomed you, or naked and gave you clothing? And when was it that we saw you sick or in prison and visited you?' And the king will answer them, 'Truly I tell you, just as you did it to one of the least of these who are members of my family, you did it to me.'"

MATTHEW 25:34–40

PRAYER

Lord of the marginalized, you yourself associated with those whom society often considered outcasts. You also had special compassion for the poor. You went as far as to tell us that we will ultimately be judged according to how we treated the least among us. Help me to reach out in a special way to those who are at the margins of society, to the poor, and to those who are otherwise seen as less-than-perfect or "undesirable."

ADVENT ACTION

Who might be considered the outcasts and marginalized in your local community, your workplace, your relationship, or perhaps in your local parish? Acknowledge these people and extend a gesture of hospitality to them. For example, invite someone to coffee or send a Christmas card to someone whom you know to be lonely.

DAY 16

The Coming Prince of Peace

We should be converted to peace; we should be converted to Christ, our peace, certain that his disarming love in the crib overcomes every dire threat and plan for violence. With confidence we need to continue to ask the Child, born of the Virgin Mary for us, that the enormous energy of his peace might drive out the hatred and revenge that lurk in the human soul. Let us ask God that the good and our love might overcome evil.

…To that end in this week let us make our prayer more intense and more persistent. *"Christus est pax nostra—Christ is our peace."* May his peace renew every angle of our daily lives. May he fill our hearts so that they will be open to the transforming action of his grace; may he pervade families so that, gathered before the crib or around the Christmas tree, they may reinforce their faithful communion; may his peace reign in cities, in nations and in the international community and spread to every corner of the globe.

JOHN PAUL II, GENERAL AUDIENCE, DECEMBER 19, 2001

THE CHILD OF PEACE

For a child has been born for us,
   a son given to us;
authority rests upon his shoulders;
   and he is named
Wonderful Counselor, Mighty God,
   Everlasting Father, Prince of Peace.
His authority shall grow continually,
   and there shall be endless peace
for the throne of David and his kingdom.
   He will establish and uphold it
with justice and with righteousness
   from this time onward and forevermore.
The zeal of the LORD of hosts will do this.

ISAIAH 9:6–7

PRAYER

Prince of Peace, we live in world beset by tension, hostility, violence, and war. While you have offered us love and life, we often choose conflict and death. We desperately long for the peace that only you can give. Only you can save us. We cannot achieve peace through our own accord. We beg you to come into our world and fill our lives and our world with your peace.

ADVENT ACTION

A prayer often attributed to Saint Francis begins, "Make me a channel of your peace." What practical step could you take today to bring Christ's peace into your own life and the world in a more visible way? Also, John Paul has urged us to pray for peace. Never doubt the power of prayer. Make peace a special intention in your prayer throughout this Advent and Christmas season.

DAY 17

The Word Through Whom All Things Were Made

John, in the Prologue of his Gospel, captures in one phrase all the depth of the mystery of the Incarnation. He writes: *"And the Word became flesh and dwelt among us, full of grace and truth; we have beheld his glory, glory as of the only Son from the Father"* (John 1:14). For John, the Incarnation of the Eternal Word, of one being with the Father, took place in the conception and birth of Jesus. The Evangelist speaks of the Word who in the beginning was with God, and through whom everything which exists was made; the Word in whom was life, the life which was the light of men (see John 1:1–4). Of the Only-Begotten Son, God from God, the Apostle Paul writes that he is *"the first-born of all creation"* (Colossians 1:15). God created the world through the Word. The Word is Eternal Wisdom; the Thought and Substantial Image of God; "He reflects the glory of God and bears the very stamp of his nature" (Hebrews 1:3). Eternally begotten and eternally loved by the Father, as God from God and Light from Light, he is the principle and archetype of everything created by God in time.

JOHN PAUL II, *TERTIO MILLENNIO ADVENIENTE*
(AS THE THIRD MILLENNIUM DRAWS NEAR), 3, NOVEMBER 10, 1994

REVELATION IN CREATION

Ever since the creation of the world his eternal power and divine nature, invisible though they are, have been understood and seen through the things he has made.

ROMANS 1:20

PRAYER

Jesus, you are the Word through whom all things were made. Creation remains a reflection of your glory and the glory of your Father. Guide me as I strive to become more attentive to the ways in which you reveal yourself through creation. This Advent, may I also reflect even more deeply on the mystery of how you, the glorious Eternal Word of God, assumed human flesh in order to renew all creation.

ADVENT ACTION

Make time to enjoy God's creation today. How does God reveal himself to you through creation? What do you learn about God through his creation? What action can you take to preserve the environment where you live?

DAY 18

Is There Room in the Inn of My Heart?

*T*he Mother of Christ teaches us to *recognize the time of God,* the favorable moment when he comes into our life and asks for a prompt and generous response. The mystery of the Holy Night, which occurred historically 2,000 years ago, becomes a reality as a spiritual event in the "*today*" of the liturgy. The Word, who took up his dwelling in Mary's womb, comes knocking at the door of every person's heart with particular intensity at this coming Christmas.

JOHN PAUL II, ANGELUS, DECEMBER 19, 1999

MARY PREPARES ROOM

The angel said to her, "Do not be afraid, Mary, for you have found favor with God. And now, you will conceive in your womb and bear a son, and you will name him Jesus. He will be great, and will be called the Son of the Most High, and the Lord God will give to him the throne of his ancestor David. He will reign over the house of

Jacob forever, and of his kingdom there will be no end." Mary said to the angel, "How can this be, since I am a virgin?" The angel said to her, "The Holy Spirit will come upon you, and the power of the Most High will overshadow you; therefore the child to be born will be holy; he will be called Son of God...." Then Mary said, "Here am I, the servant of the Lord; let it be with me according to your word."

LUKE 1:30–35, 38

PRAYER

Jesus, your mother, in an act of unconditional surrender to the will of God, made room for you in her life. The Gospel of Luke tells me that at the moment of your birth, there was no room for your family in the inn and that you, therefore, came into the world in a manger (2:7). At your coming this Christmas, I want to be sure that there is room for you in my heart. May this Advent season be one in which I clear space for you in my life so that you may have accommodation truly befitting your presence.

ADVENT ACTION

What clutter do you need to get rid of in your life to make room for Christ's coming? As an act symbolic of preparing room in your heart for Christ, give up a guilty pleasure today. For example, turn off the television for an hour when you would have ordinarily watched it and spend the time with a friend or family member, or on spiritual reading, or in prayer. Turn over any cares or worries that are occupying your heart to God.

DAY 19

Suffering and God's Plan of Salvation

*E*ven though the victory over sin and death achieved by Christ in his Cross and Resurrection does not abolish temporal suffering from human life…it nevertheless *throws a new light* upon this dimension and upon every suffering: the light of salvation. This is the light of the Gospel, that is, of the Good News. At the heart of this light is the truth expounded in the conversation with Nicodemus: "For God so loved the world that he gave his only Son" (John 3:16). This truth radically changes the picture of man's history and his earthly situation: …God the Father has loved the only-begotten Son, that is, he loves him in a lasting way; and then in time, precisely through this all-surpassing love, he "gives" this Son, that he may strike at the very roots of human evil and thus draw close in a salvific way to the whole world of suffering in which man shares.

JOHN PAUL II, *SALVIFICI DOLORIS*
(ON THE CHRISTIAN MEANING OF HUMAN SUFFERING),
15, FEBRUARY 11, 1984

Faithful Endurance

As for you, always be sober, endure suffering, do the work of an evangelist, carry out your ministry fully.

As for me, I am already being poured out as a libation, and the time of my departure has come. I have fought the good fight, I have finished the race, I have kept the faith. From now on there is reserved for me the crown of righteousness, which the Lord, the righteous judge, will give me on that day, and not only to me but also to all who have longed for his appearing.

2 Timothy 4:5–8

Prayer

Lord Jesus, you took on human flesh in order to show your love for humankind and to enter into, embrace, and transform human suffering. Help me to face my suffering by seeing it as united with your own redemptive suffering. May I draw closer to you through my experience of suffering and by reaching out to others who suffer. I look forward to the day when your kingdom will be brought to fulfillment and there will be no more tears, suffering, or dying (see Revelation 21:4).

Advent Action

Reflect on how you have drawn closer to God and others through the suffering you have endured in your life. Be an agent of Christ's salvific presence in the world by doing something to alleviate (if only a small way) someone's physical, psychological, or emotional suffering. Make a plan to visit a nursing home this Advent. Be sure to reach out to those who might otherwise not receive visitors.

DAY 20

Being vs. Doing

*O*urs is a time of continual movement which often leads to restlessness, with the risk of "doing for the sake of doing." We must resist this temptation by trying "to be" before trying "to do." In this regard we should recall how Jesus reproved Martha: "You are anxious and troubled about many things; one thing is needful" (Luke 10:41–42).

JOHN PAUL II, *NOVO MILLENNIO INEUNTE*
(AT THE BEGINNING OF THE NEW MILLENNIUM), 15,
JANUARY 6, 2001

BEING LIKE CHILDREN

At that time the disciples came to Jesus and asked, "Who is the greatest in the kingdom of heaven?" He called a child, whom he put among them, and said, "Truly I tell you, unless you change and become like children, you will never enter the kingdom of heaven. Whoever becomes humble like this child is the greatest in the kingdom of heaven."

MATTHEW 18:1–4

PRAYER

Lord, as I prepare for Christmas, it is easy to get so caught up in "doing" things that I often forget to take time just to be present to you, my family, and other loved ones. Help me to keep my priorities in line. This means keeping my focus on what is most important: you. Let me be like a child who simply rejoices in being with you. Remind me that the more I simply relish being in your presence, the closer I will come to you this Advent.

ADVENT ACTION

Take your Christmas to-do list (either mental or written out) and cross off one task that is not absolutely necessary. Use that time to be present to God, family, or friends.

DAY 21

O Antiphons

*L*ike ancient Israel, the Church speaks for the men and women of all time as she sings the Advent of the Savior. From day to day she prays, *"O Wisdom that comes forth from the mouth of the Most High," "O Guide of the House of Israel," "O Root of Jesse," "O Key of David," "O Rising Sun, O Sun of Justice," "O King of the nations," "O Emmanuel, God-with-us."*

In each of these fervent appeals, full of biblical references, one finds the ardent desire that believers have to see completed their waiting for peace. For this reason one implores the gift of the birth of the promised Savior. At the same time however one sees clearly that it entails a concrete effort to prepare a worthy dwelling place not just in their souls, but also in the setting around them. In a word, if we ask Him who brings peace into the world to come, that entails opening ourselves docilely to the renewing truth and power of the Gospel.

JOHN PAUL II, GENERAL AUDIENCE, DECEMBER 19, 2001

The Promised One

> *For a child has been born for us,*
> *a son given to us;*
> *authority rests upon his shoulders;*
> *and he is named*
> *Wonderful Counselor, Mighty God,*
> *Everlasting Father, Prince of Peace.*

Isaiah 9:6

Prayer

Lord God, through the prophets of old you promised your people a savior, an anointed one, a messiah. People in both the past and the present have looked to earthly rulers for solutions to their problems. The savior whom you offer us, however, is not a political power but the gift of yourself in the person of your own Son. It is he whom we await with eager anticipation. You are as faithful to your promises today as you were to your promises of old. May the long-awaited One fill our world with love, peace, wisdom, and truth this holy season. Come, Lord Jesus.

Advent Action

What title (or "O Antiphon") would you give to the coming Christ child? Create a title that has personal significance to you and use it in prayer this Advent. Keep a copy of your antiphon in your pocket as a reminder to pray it throughout the day.

DAY 22

The Coming Christ Child: Our Cause for Hope

Advent keeps alive our expectation of Christ who will come to visit us with his salvation, fully establishing his Kingdom of justice and peace. The annual evocation of the Messiah's birth in Bethlehem renews in believers' hearts the certainty that God keeps his promises. Advent is, therefore, *a powerful proclamation of hope*, which deeply touches our personal and communitarian experience.

Every man and woman dreams of a more just and supportive world where a dignified standard of life and peaceful coexistence harmonize relations between individuals and peoples. All too often, however, this is not the case. Obstacles, disputes and difficulties of various kinds burden our life and sometimes almost overwhelm it.…It is especially at these moments that hope comes to our rescue. The mystery of Christmas…assures us that God is the *Emmanuel—God-with-us.* This is why we must never feel alone. He is close to us, he became one of us, born from the virginal womb of Mary. He shared our pilgrimage on earth, guaranteeing us the attainment of that joy and peace to which we aspire from the depths of our being.

JOHN PAUL II, GENERAL AUDIENCE, DECEMBER 17, 2003

WAITING IN HOPE

We know that the whole creation has been groaning in labor pains until now; and not only the creation, but we ourselves, who have the first fruits of the Spirit, groan inwardly while we wait for adoption, the redemption of our bodies. For in hope we were saved. Now hope that is seen is not hope. For who hopes for what is seen? But if we hope for what we do not see, we wait for it with patience.

ROMANS 8:22–25

PRAYER

Lord, often it just seems as if the world is moving away from you and in the wrong direction. As I get older, it is easy to become cynical and to believe that hope is a childish concept. Yet I am told to hope in you (Psalm 130:7). You entered the world to be with and to give reason for hope to your people. I am confident that you can and will make the world a better place. If to have hope is to be a child, then let me be your child. Give me the confidence to place my hope in you.

ADVENT ACTIVITY

How has the Lord met or surpassed your hopes, even in ways that you did not expect? Reflect on what it is that you hope for. Entrust these hopes to the coming Christ child while meditating in the presence of a Nativity scene or other religious symbol in your home.

DAY 23

Advent: A Time to Rejoice

Rejoice in the Lord always" [Philippians 4:4]. In the face of the inevitable difficulties of life, the uncertainties and fears for the future, the temptation to give in to despair and disappointment, the Word of God always proclaims again the "*glad tidings*" of salvation: the Son of God comes to heal "*the wounds of the broken-hearted*" (see Isaiah 61:1). May this joy, anticipation of the coming joy of Christmas, fill each of our hearts and every corner of our lives.

JOHN PAUL II, HOMILY, MASS WITH THE COMMUNITY
OF ST. JOHN NEPOMUCENE PARISH, DECEMBER 15, 2002

REJOICE! OUR KING IS COMING

Rejoice greatly, O daughter Zion!
Shout aloud, O daughter Jerusalem!
Lo, your king comes to you;
triumphant and victorious is he....

ZECHARIAH 9:9

PRAYER

God, you know that I carry a number of worries, concerns, and hurts. It is particularly easy to get weighed down with these burdens during the dark days of winter. Yet, you reassure me that my King, my salvation, is coming. Truly this is a reason to rejoice. During these days of anticipation as I await the coming of your Son, help me to remember that now is a time to rejoice.

ADVENT ACTION

Look around you. What in your life is definitely a source of rejoicing? In anticipation of the Lord's coming, rejoice in a special way today by allowing yourself a special treat or indulgence. Also, make a point of not taking so seriously those things that do not merit seriousness. Rejoice in the gift of laughter.

DAY 24

Restored to Our Dignity through the Incarnation

We also are in a certain way in a season of a new Advent, a season of expectation: "In many and various ways God spoke of old to our fathers by the prophets; but in these last days he has spoken to us by a Son…" (Hebrews 1:1–2), by the Son, his Word, who became man and was born of the Virgin Mary. This act of redemption marked the high point of the history of man within God's loving plan. God entered the history of humanity and, as a man, became an actor in that history, one of the thousands of millions of human beings but at the same time Unique! Through the Incarnation God gave human life the dimension that he intended man to have from his first beginning; he has granted that dimension definitively—in the way that is peculiar to him alone, in keeping with his eternal love and mercy….

JOHN PAUL II, *REDEMPTOR HOMINIS*
(THE REDEEMER OF MAN), 1, MARCH 4, 1978

MADE WHOLE AGAIN

The scribes and the Pharisees brought a woman who had been caught in adultery; and making her stand before all of them, they said to him, "Teacher, this woman was caught in the very act of committing adultery. Now in the law Moses commanded us to stone such women. Now what do you say?"...[He] said to them, "Let anyone among you who is without sin be the first to throw a stone at her." When they heard it, they went away, one by one, beginning with the elders; and Jesus was left alone with the woman standing before him. Jesus...said to her, "Woman, where are they? Has no one condemned you?" She said, "No one, sir." And Jesus said, "Neither do I condemn you. Go your way, and from now on do not sin again."

JOHN 8:3–5, 7, 9–11

PRAYER

Jesus, when we fall short of the dignity to which we are called, you do what we cannot do on our own: You pick us up, restore our dignity, and help us to continue on our journey of becoming the kind of people you want us to be. You have great plans for me and all people. Help me to be ever mindful of your great love for me and the dignity to which you call me.

ADVENT ACTION

Do you fall into the habit of putting yourself down when you make a mistake? Recognize that God sent his Son to pick you up, not to put you down. Today when you make a mistake or fall short of the dignity to which God calls you, rather than putting yourself down, remember God's love for you and ask for the grace to become the person he is calling you to be. Also, when you encounter someone who has "fallen" today, rather than being critical, be Christ's agent by helping to pick up him or her.

DAY 25

Remembering the True Meaning of Christmas

*L*et us pause to contemplate the Grotto of Bethlehem. The King of the universe did not even have that indispensable minimum which every family prepares in advance for a child's birth and Mary and Joseph, for whom there was no room at the inn, were obliged to seek shelter in a humble stable.

The manger would be the first cradle of the newborn Child (see Luke 2:7). Therefore God became one of us in a setting of extreme poverty....

This scene, in its simplicity, is a silent invitation to understand the true value of the Christmas mystery, a mystery of humility and love, of joy and of attention to the poor.

While people in their homes are putting the finishing touches to their cribs and are preparing to spend Christmas in serene family harmony, may they not overlook an act of solidarity for those who will unfortunately spend these days in loneliness and suffering. The joy of this feast will be all the greater the more we are able to share it, not only with our family and friends, but also with all those who expect a concrete remembrance from us.

JOHN PAUL II, ANGELUS, DECEMBER 24, 2000

BLESSINGS ON THE POOR

Then he looked up at his disciples and said:
   "Blessed are you who are poor,
      for yours is the kingdom of God.
   "Blessed are you who are hungry now,
      for you will be filled.
   "Blessed are you who weep now,
      for you will laugh.
"Blessed are you when people hate you, and when they exclude you, revile you, and defame you on account of the Son of Man. Rejoice in that day and leap for joy, for surely your reward is great in heaven...."

LUKE 6:20–23

PRAYER

Lord Jesus, as I get caught up in my own Christmas preparations, I easily forget those who will go without this season. Help me to remember in a special way the poor, with whom you have always been intimately connected since your own birth in a stable. By remembering them, I am truly giving honor to you.

ADVENT ACTION

Volunteer with a charitable organization or in a church program that seeks to create a Merry Christmas for the disadvantaged. If you are not able to participate in person, make a charitable donation.

DAY 26

The Dignity of All Human Life

A special commitment is needed with regard to certain aspects of the Gospel's radical message which are often less well understood, even to the point of making the Church's presence unpopular, but which nevertheless must be a part of her mission of charity. I am speaking of the duty to be committed to *respect for the life of every human being,* from conception until natural death. Likewise, the service of humanity leads us to insist, in season and out of season, that those using *the latest advances of science,* especially in the field of biotechnology, must never disregard fundamental ethical requirements by invoking a questionable solidarity which eventually leads to discriminating between one life and another and ignoring the dignity which belongs to every human being.

JOHN PAUL II, *NOVO MILLENNIO INEUNTE*
(AT THE BEGINNING OF THE NEW MILLENNIUM), 51, JANUARY 6, 2001

CHOOSING LIFE

I have set before you life and death, blessings and curses. Choose life so that you and your descendants may live....

DEUTERONOMY 30:19

PRAYER

Lord Jesus, during this Advent season I eagerly anticipate the arrival of new life. You reaffirmed the value of human life by becoming human yourself. Foster in me a deeper respect for all human life—especially that which society would deem less than perfect—from the moment of conception to the point of natural death. Let me welcome and embrace all human life with the same love that your own mother welcomed and embraced you on that night in Bethlehem. Teach me to reach out to the poor, sick, and the outcasts as you did in your own earthly ministry.

ADVENT ACTION

What can you do to promote greater respect for the dignity of all human life? Perhaps there is a sick or elderly friend or relative whom you could visit or call today or consider other affronts to the dignity of human life, such as abortion, war, and capital punishment. Make your voice heard when you see or hear others degrading the value of human life in any of its stages. Take action today by becoming involved in or supporting an organization that promotes respect for the dignity of human life.

DAY 27

God's Mercy in the World

*I*n this way, the messianic message about mercy preserves a
particular divine-human dimension. Christ—the very
fulfillment of the messianic prophecy—by becoming the
incarnation of the love that is manifested with particular force
with regard to the suffering, the unfortunate and sinners, makes
present and thus more fully reveals the Father, who is God "rich
in mercy." At the same time, by becoming for people a model of
merciful love for others, Christ proclaims by His actions even
more than by His words that call to mercy which is one of the
essential elements of the Gospel ethos. In this instance it is not
just a case of fulfilling a commandment or an obligation of an
ethical nature; it is also a case of satisfying a condition of major
importance for God to reveal Himself in His mercy to man: "The
merciful…shall obtain mercy."

JOHN PAUL II, *DIVES IN MISERICORDIA*
(RICH IN MERCY), 3, NOVEMBER 30, 1980

Trusting in the Lord's Mercy

Therefore the LORD waits to be gracious to you;
therefore he will rise up to show mercy to you.
For the LORD is a God of justice;
blessed are all those who wait for him.
Truly, O people in Zion, inhabitants of Jerusalem, you shall
weep no more. He will surely be gracious to you at the sound
of your cry; when he hears it, he will answer you.

ISAIAH 30:18–19

Prayer

Lord Jesus, you came to show us your Father's loving mercy. Fortunately, you do not treat us as we deserve but love us even when we fail and abuse the freedom with which we have been endowed. In turn, help me to go beyond justice in dealing with others so that I might reach out to them in true Christian love. May I show mercy to others as you have shown mercy to me.

Advent Action

Be an instrument of God's mercy today. Forgive a wrong committed against you without complaint and without expecting recompense. Seek to strengthen relationships in your life by letting go of a grievance.

DAY 28

O Holy Night

On this Holy Night the ancient promise is fulfilled: the time of waiting has ended and the Virgin gives birth to the Messiah.

On this night God answers the ceaseless cry of the peoples: Come, Lord, save us! His eternal Word of love has taken on our mortal flesh. "Your Word, O Lord, came down from his royal throne." The Word has entered into time: Emmanuel, God-with-us, is born.

Jesus is born for a humanity searching for freedom and peace; he is born for everyone burdened by sin, in need of salvation, and yearning for hope....

Mary "gave birth to her first-born son and wrapped him in swaddling cloths, and laid him in a manger" (Luke 2:7).

This is the icon of Christmas: a tiny newborn child, whom the hands of a woman wrap in poor cloths and lay in a manger.

Who could imagine that this little human being is the "Son of the Most High" (Luke 1:32)? Only she, his Mother, knows the truth and guards its mystery.

On this night we too can "join" in her gaze and so recognize in this Child the human face of God. We too—the men and women of the third millennium—are able to encounter Christ and to gaze upon him through the eyes of Mary.

Christmas night thus becomes a school of faith and of life.

JOHN PAUL II, HOMILY,
MIDNIGHT MASS, CHRISTMAS, DECEMBER 24, 2002

THE HEAVEN-SENT MESSAGE

…[T]he angel said to [the shepherds], "Do not be afraid; for see— I am bringing you good news of great joy for all the people: to you is born this day in the city of David a Savior, who is the Messiah, the Lord. This will be a sign for you: you will find a child wrapped in bands of cloth and lying in a manger."

LUKE 2:10–12

PRAYER

This evening, I welcome you, Jesus, in the most unpretentious of forms: that of a baby. Truly I discover this evening that the greatest of gifts can come in the simplest of wrappings. How can I thank you for the gift of yourself, the Word of God having taken on human flesh as a baby in a manger? The best I can do is to give you my love…and that is what I present you with this evening.

ADVENT ACTIVITY

Amid the hustle and bustle of Christmas Eve preparations, take a moment to pray in the presence of a Nativity scene or picture of the Christ child. As a symbol of your baptism and your acceptance of the Incarnation, light a candle near the Nativity scene or picture. Continue to use the candle as part of your prayer throughout the Christmas season.

Readings for the Christmas Season

DAY 1

Infant Savior

In the heavens there echoes the proclamation of the angels: *"To you is born in the city of David a Savior, who is Christ the Lord"* (Luke 2:11). What wonder! By being born in Bethlehem, the Eternal Son of God has *entered into the history of each person living* on the face of the earth. He is now present in the world as the one Savior of humanity. For this reason we pray to him: *Savior of the world, save us!*

Save us from the great evils which rend humanity in these first years of the third millennium. Save us from the wars and armed conflicts which lay waste whole areas of the world, from the scourge of terrorism and from the many forms of violence which assail the weak and the vulnerable. Save us from discouragement as we face the paths to peace, difficult paths indeed, yet possible and therefore necessary; paths which are always and everywhere urgent, especially in the Land where You were born, the Prince of Peace.

JOHN PAUL II, *URBI ET ORBI*, CHRISTMAS 2003

OUTPOURING OF THE SPIRIT THROUGH THE SAVIOR

For we ourselves were once foolish, disobedient, led astray, slaves to various passions and pleasures, passing our days in malice and envy, despicable, hating one another. But when the goodness and loving kindness of God our Savior appeared, he saved us, not because of any works of righteousness that we had done, but according to his mercy, through the water of rebirth and renewal by the Holy Spirit. This Spirit he poured out on us richly through Jesus Christ our Savior, so that, having been justified by his grace, we might become heirs according to the hope of eternal life. The saying is sure.

TITUS 3:3–8

PRAYER

Infant Jesus, it is with awe that I contemplate how you, a tiny baby, are our Savior. It is you who can rescue the world from threats of violence and despair. You can save us from ourselves and give meaning to our lives. Keep me ever mindful that in you I can find all the strength and power necessary to face whatever it is in my life that may threaten or challenge me. Today, I welcome you, oh long-awaited Savior.

CHRISTMAS ACTION

Take a moment to contemplate what it is that you long to be saved from and saved for. What is it that you feel most threatened by? Entrust these cares to the Christ child, your Savior. As a sign of recognition that your Savior has come, allow yourself to let go of worries and be relaxed today. Allow yourself to be fully present to family members and loved ones.

DAY 2

Remaining Firm in Faith: The Example of Saint Stephen

The first of the martyrs is Saint Stephen, whose feast we are celebrating today. He gave his life as a witness of his loyalty to the Redeemer. In the darkness of persecution, the Lord appeared to him like the radiant star which, by overcoming the shadow of evil, rekindles hope and proclaims the new dawn: eternal life.

Thus the memory of the Protomartyr Stephen in a certain sense extends the joy of Christmas. His courageous and faithful option for Jesus encourages us to bear a consistent witness to the Gospel, as did he who, filled with the Holy Spirit, followed Christ and imitated him in life and death. May his example sustain in particular those who, today too, are subjected to harsh trials because of their faith, so that they will never lack the courage to give the Lord their total support.

JOHN PAUL II, ANGELUS, FEAST OF SAINT STEPHEN,
DECEMBER 26, 1998

THE FIRST MARTYR

[And Stephen said,] "You stiff-necked people, uncircumcised in heart and ears, you are forever opposing the Holy Spirit, just as your ancestors used to do...."

When they heard these things, they became enraged and ground their teeth at Stephen.... Then they dragged him out of the city and began to stone him; and the witnesses laid their coats at the feet of a young man named Saul. While they were stoning Stephen, he prayed, "Lord Jesus, receive my spirit." Then he knelt down and cried out in a loud voice, "Lord, do not hold this sin against them." When he had said this, he died.

ACTS 7:51, 54, 58–60

PRAYER

Lord, Stephen faithfully witnessed to the gospel to the point of giving his life. Strengthen me with the virtue of fortitude. Inspired by the hope and joy of this Christmas season, may I too persevere in being a witness to you even when I face adversity or persecution for doing so.

CHRISTMAS ACTION

Work at developing the virtue of fortitude. Is there something you have been putting off doing out of fear? Face it with courage today. Is there a challenge you face over which you are becoming discouraged? Are you considering giving up? Strengthened by Christ, make an effort to persevere in this endeavor. Today, when you hesitate to take the correct course of action because of fear, ask Christ for the strength to do the right thing.

DAY 3

The Bread Come Down From Heaven

*I*n the *Son of the Virgin*, "wrapped in swaddling clothes and lying in a manger" (Luke 2:12), we acknowledge and adore *"the Bread which came down from heaven"* (John 6:41, 51), the Redeemer who came among us in order to bring life to the world.

Bethlehem! The city where Jesus was born in fulfillment of the Scriptures, in Hebrew means *"house of bread."* It was there that the Messiah was to be born, the One who would say of himself: "I am the bread of life" (John 6:35, 48).

In Bethlehem was born the One who, under the sign of broken bread, would leave us the memorial of his Pasch. On this Holy Night, adoration of the Child Jesus becomes *Eucharistic adoration.*

We adore you, Lord, truly present in the Sacrament of the Altar, the living Bread which gives life to humanity. We acknowledge you as *our one God*, a little Child lying helpless in the manger! "In the fullness of time, you became a man among men, to unite the end to the beginning, that is, man to God" (see Saint Irenaeus, *Adversus Haereses*, IV, 20, 4).

JOHN PAUL II, HOMILY, MIDNIGHT MASS, DECEMBER 24, 2004

LIVING BREAD

"I am the bread of life. Your ancestors ate the manna in the wilderness, and they died. This is the bread that comes down from heaven, so that one may eat of it and not die. I am the living bread that came down from heaven. Whoever eats of this bread will live forever; and the bread that I will give for the life of the world is my flesh."

JOHN 6:48–51

PRAYER

Lord Jesus, you are life-giving bread come down from heaven. In the manger lies the life of the world. Be my food. Nourish me and sustain me throughout my journey here on earth. During this Christmas season, may I grow evermore appreciative of the gift of your presence with us in the Eucharist.

CHRISTMAS ACTION

Take time today or this week to pray before Jesus present in the Eucharist in the tabernacle. Reflect on how the babe of the manger truly is life for the world.

DAY 4

Following the Star

*H*ow striking is the *symbol of the star* that recurs in all the images of Christmas and Epiphany! It still gives rise to deep feelings although, as with so many other sacred signs, it risks becoming common place because of its commercial overuse. Restored to its original context, the star we contemplate over the crib *also speaks to the mind and heart of the man of the third millennium.* It speaks to secularized man, awakening in him the nostalgia of his condition as pilgrim in search of the truth with a *deep desire for the absolute....*

Who does not feel the need for a "star" to guide him on his earthly journey? Individuals and nations both feel the need....

The oracle of the Prophet Isaiah...rings out for the entire ecclesial community: *"Arise, shine; for your light has come, and the glory of the Lord has risen upon you....And nations shall come to your light, and kings to the brightness of your rising"* (Isaiah 60:1, 3)....

Do not be afraid of the darkness of the world, because the one who is calling you is *"the light of the world"* (John 8:12), *"the bright morning star"* (Revelation 22:16).

JOHN PAUL II, HOMILY, SOLEMNITY OF THE EPIPHANY, JANUARY 6, 2002

WALKING IN THE LIGHT

For once you were darkness, but now in the Lord you are light. Live as children of light—for the fruit of the light is found in all that is good and right and true. Try to find out what is pleasing to the Lord. Take no part in the unfruitful works of darkness, but instead expose them.... Therefore it says,

> *"Sleeper, awake!*
>   *Rise from the dead,*
>   *and Christ will shine on you."*

EPHESIANS 5:8–11, 14

PRAYER

Christ, in a world that often appears cloaked in darkness, I need a light to lead me to the truth. There are many lights that dazzle me and compete for my attention. Help me not to become distracted. You alone are the light that I must follow to find meaning in my life. Be my star. Lead me to the truth that is you.

CHRISTMAS ACTION

We are to be light for the world, leading others to God (see Matthew 5:14–16). How can you reflect Christ's light to others? Are you a bright beacon or a dim bulb? Be positive in your dealings with others today, letting Christ's life that is within you shine through. Bring Christ's lightby extending a gesture of kindness to someone who is, for whatever reason, wrapped in darkness.

DAY 5

Faith at the Center of the Family

The message that comes from the Holy Family is first of all a message of *faith*: the family of Nazareth is a home which truly centers on God. For Mary and Joseph, this choice of faith becomes concrete in their service to the Son of God entrusted to their care, but it is also expressed in their mutual love, rich in spiritual tenderness and fidelity.

With their life, they teach that marriage is *a covenant between man and woman*, a covenant that involves *reciprocal fidelity* and rests upon *their common trust in God*. Such a noble, profound and definitive covenant, as to constitute for believers the sacrament of love of Christ and of the Church. The spouses' fidelity stands like a *solid rock on which the children's trust rests*.

When parents and children together breathe this atmosphere of faith they have a ready energy that enables them to face even difficult trials, as the Holy Family's experience shows.

JOHN PAUL II, ANGELUS,
FEAST OF THE HOLY FAMILY, DECEMBER 29, 1996

A "Real-World" Family of Love

When his parents saw him [in the Temple] they were astonished; and his mother said to him, "Child, why have you treated us like this? Look, your father and I have been searching for you in great anxiety." He said to them, "Why were you searching for me? Did you not know that I must be in my Father's house?" But they did not understand what he said to them. Then he went down with them and came to Nazareth, and was obedient to them. His mother treasured all these things in her heart.

And Jesus increased in wisdom and in years, and in divine and human favor.

LUKE 2:48–52

Prayer

Lord Jesus, at times my family can seem pretty dysfunctional. Yet, I know no family is without problems. Your family, too, had challenges to face. Be with my family, however spread out we may be and wherever we may be on our own faith journeys. Help us to recognize that we will be able to face the challenges that confront us only if we put you at the center of our lives.

Christmas Action

We've all heard it: The family that prays together stays together. Take the opportunity to pray together as a family today, perhaps at mealtime. Ask Christ to unite your family in deeper love. If, for whatever reason, you are unable to pray with your family, look through a family photo album and pray for your family members, living and deceased.

DAY 6

Changed Lives

*L*et us pause, in a special way, to contemplate *the shepherds.* Simple and joyful models of our human searching,…they highlight the interior conditions required to meet Jesus.

The disarming tenderness of the Child, the surprising poverty in which he is found and the humble simplicity of Mary and Joseph transform the shepherds' lives: thus they become messengers of salvation, evangelists *ante litteram* [before the letter]. Saint Luke writes: "the shepherds returned, glorifying and praising God for all they had heard and seen, as it had been told them" (Luke 2:20). They left happy and enriched by an event that had changed their lives. In their words is the echo of an inner joy which becomes praise: "they returned, glorifying and praising God."

JOHN PAUL II, HOMILY, SOLEMNITY OF MARY,
MOTHER OF GOD, XXXIV WORLD DAY OF PEACE, JANUARY 1, 2001

CHANGED THROUGH AN ENCOUNTER WITH CHRIST

When the angels had left them and gone into heaven, the shepherds said to one another, "Let us go now to Bethlehem and see this thing that has taken place, which the Lord has made known to us." So they went with haste and found Mary and Joseph, and he child lying in the manger. When they saw this, they made known what had been told them about this child; and all who heard it were amazed at what the shepherds told them. But Mary treasured all these words and pondered them in her heart. The shepherds returned, glorifying and praising God for all they had heard and seen, as it had been told them.

LUKE 2:15–20

PRAYER

Lord, your birth was first announced to poor, simple shepherds lying in a field. After visiting you in the manger, their lives were transformed by your glory. How could they ever be the same after having encountered you, God-become-man? May my life likewise be transformed by my encounter with you in that humble stable this Christmas and by all the encounters with you in my life.

CHRISTMAS ACTION

At the beginning of Advent, you wrote down your hopes and goals for the season. How have you done at realizing them? How has your life been changed through your encounter with Christ this Christmas? What can you do in the new year to better demonstrate your life-altering encounter with Christ?

Like the shepherds, praise God in a special way today for the gift of his Son and for the wonders he works in your own life. Be an agent of joy to those around you.

God in Time

Te Deum laudamus! [We praise you, God!] Thus does the Church sing her gratitude to God, while she is still rejoicing at the Lord's Birth....[O]ur attention is attracted by the *ideal convergence of the solar year with the liturgical year,* two temporal cycles that underlie two dimensions of time.

In the first dimension, the days, months and years succeed one another in a cosmic rhythm in which the human mind recognizes the imprint of the divine creative Wisdom. This is why the Church exclaims: *Te Deum laudamus!*

The other dimension of time...is that of the history of salvation. At its center and summit is the mystery of Christ. The Apostle Paul...[reminds] us of it: "*When the time had fully come, God sent forth his Son*" (Galatians 4:4). Christ is the center of history and of the cosmos; he is the new Sun that dawned upon the world from "*on high*" (Luke 1:78), a Sun that directs all things to the ultimate goal of history.

In these days between Christmas and New Year's Day, these

two dimensions of time intersect with special eloquence. It is as though the eternity of God had come to visit human time. The Eternal thus becomes a present "instant" so that the cyclical repetition of days and years does not end in a senseless void.

JOHN PAUL II, HOMILY, *TE DEUM* AND FIRST VESPERS OF THE SOLEMNITY OF MARY, MOTHER OF GOD, DECEMBER 31, 2003

TODAY IS THE DAY OF SALVATION

As we work together with him, we urge you also not to accept the grace of God in vain. For he says,
"At an acceptable time I have listened to you,
and on a day of salvation I have helped you."
See, now is the acceptable time; see, now is the day of salvation!

2 CORINTHIANS 6:1–2

PRAYER

God of all time, you sent your Son, the Eternal Word, into our "human time" for the salvation of the world. Today, in a special way I mark the passage of time. I celebrate the end of one year and thank you for the gift of life in it. I look forward to the many blessings I will experience in the coming year and pray that you will be with me in whatever trials I may face.

CHRISTMAS ACTION

Time is a valuable gift. How can you make the most of your time in the coming year? Is there a way you could reduce wasted time in order to make more time for God in your life? Make a practical, achievable resolution to spend more time with God in prayer in the new year. Determine specifically how you plan to achieve this goal. Write it down!

DAY 8

Mary, Mother of God

A humble creature conceived the Creator of the world! The liturgical season of Christmas renews our awareness of this mystery, presenting to us the Mother of the Son of God as sharing in the crowning events of the history of salvation. The age-old tradition of the Church has always considered the birth of Jesus and the divine motherhood of Mary as two aspects of the Incarnation of the Word....

In these last days of the Christmas season, let us pause to contemplate in the Nativity scene *the silent presence of the Virgin beside the Baby Jesus.* She lavishes on us the same love, the same care that she lavished on her divine Son. Let us therefore allow her to guide our steps in this *new year* that Providence has granted us to live....Sustained and comforted by her maternal protection, we will be able to contemplate the face of Christ with a renewed gaze, and walk more swiftly on the paths of good.

JOHN PAUL II, GENERAL AUDIENCE, JANUARY 7, 2004
(REFLECTION ON THE SOLEMNITY OF MARY, MOTHER OF GOD)

Following Mary's Guidance

On the third day there was a wedding in Cana of Galilee, and the mother of Jesus was there. Jesus and his disciples had also been invited to the wedding. When the wine gave out, the mother of Jesus said to him, "They have no wine." And Jesus said to her, "Woman, what concern is that to you and to me? My hour has not yet come." His mother said to the servants, "Do whatever he tells you."

JOHN 2:1–5

Prayer

Mary, loving Mother of God and my own mother, you bring my needs before your Son Jesus, with whom you share a most special relationship. In this new year, I ask you to lead me closer to him. Help me to gaze upon his face with the same love, wonder, and devotion that you did. May I have the strength, courage, and conviction to become more like you in following his will in my own life. Mother of the Incarnate Word, be with me, intercede for me, and continue to inspire me by your own example.

Christmas Action

Reflect on how you wish to become more like Mary, Model of Discipleship, in the coming year. What characteristics of Mary are you in most need of in your own life: courage, faithfulness, gentleness, openness, trust, prayerfulness? Make it your New Year's resolution to work at fostering this characteristic in your own life. Write down your resolution and, if practical, let others know of it.

DAY 9

The Gift of Love

Christmas is a mystery of love! The love of the Father, who has sent into the world his only-begotten Son, to bestow on us the gift of his own life (see 1 John 4:8–9). The love of "God-with-us," Emmanuel, who came to earth in order to die on the Cross. In the cold stable, wrapped in silence, the Virgin Mother, with prophetic intuition, already tastes the violent drama of Calvary, the traumatic struggle between darkness and light, between death and life, between hatred and love. The Prince of Peace, born today in Bethlehem, will give his life on Golgotha, so that love may reign on earth.

JOHN PAUL II, *URBI ET ORBI*, CHRISTMAS 2002

GOD'S GREAT LOVE

Beloved, let us love one another, because love is from God; everyone who loves is born of God and knows God. Whoever does not love does not know God, for God is love. God's love was revealed among us in this way: God sent his only Son into the world so that we might live through him. In this is love, not that we loved God but that he loved us and sent his Son to be the atoning sacrifice for our sins. Beloved, since God loved us so much, we also ought to love one another. No one has ever seen God; if we love one another, God lives in us, and his love is perfected in us.

1 JOHN 4:7–12

PRAYER

Lord God, in the greatest display of your love for me, you gave me the gift of your Son. It is this child who ultimately conquered sin and death by pouring out his own life for love of me and all people. While in this world I will never fully comprehend the mystery of this great love, may my own life always be a reflection of your love to the world. May your heartbeat become mine.

CHRISTMAS ACTION

God let his love for us be known. Our love for others should not remain an unspoken secret. Too often, we do not let loved ones know that we love them. Speak the words. Let someone—someone you ordinarily do not inform of your love—know that you love him or her.

DAY 10

The Music of Christmas:
The Song of God's Victory

*H*ow many expressive songs has Christmas inspired in every people and culture! Who has not known the emotions they express? Their melodies bring alive once more the mystery of the Holy Night; they tell of the encounter between the Gospel and the paths of mankind. Yes, Christmas has entered the hearts of the peoples, who look to Bethlehem with shared wonderment....

How can we fail to notice the strident contrast between the serenity of the Christmas carols and the many problems of the present hour? We know the disturbing developments from the reports coming each day from television and the newspapers, sweeping from one hemisphere to the other of the globe....

May the joy of Christmas, which sings of the birth of the Savior, instill in all trust in the power of truth and of patient perseverance in doing good. For each of us the divine message of Bethlehem resounds: "Be not afraid; for behold, I bring you good news of a great joy, to you is born this day in the city of David a Savior, who is Christ the Lord" (Luke 2:10–11).

JOHN PAUL II, *URBI ET ORBI*, CHRISTMAS 1998

SING OF THE LORD'S GLORY

> *Sing to the LORD, all the earth.*
> *Tell of his salvation from day to day.*
> *Declare his glory among the nations,*
> *his marvelous works among all the peoples.*

1 CHRONICLES 16:23–24

PRAYER

Lord, let the music of Christmas lift my soul and lead me to deeper contemplation of the awesomeness of your Incarnation. Your birth certainly is cause for great rejoicing. May the carols of Christmas ever remind me of your closeness to me, your ability to relate to my humanness, the depth of your great love, and your ultimate victory over all that plagues the world.

CHRISTMAS ACTION

Don't put away your Christmas music the day after Christmas! Find a moment to be alone and listen to one of your favorite Christmas hymns. What does the hymn tell you about the mystery of the Incarnation and of God's love for you? Contemplate the words of the hymn and allow the song's message to touch your heart. While some might find it strange, feel free to listen to Christmas music outside of the Christmas season. Christmas hymns are excellent guides for reflecting on the mystery of the Incarnation anytime of the year.

DAY 11

Diversity and Dialogue

*I*ndividuals come to maturity through receptive openness to others and through generous self-giving to them; so too do cultures....

In this perspective, *dialogue between cultures...emerges as an intrinsic demand of human nature itself, as well as of culture.* It is dialogue which protects the distinctiveness of cultures as historical and creative expressions of the underlying unity of the human family, and which sustains understanding and communion between them....

Dialogue leads to a recognition of diversity and opens the mind to the mutual acceptance and genuine collaboration demanded by the human family's basic vocation to unity. As such, dialogue is a privileged means for building *the civilization of love and peace....*

JOHN PAUL II, MESSAGE FOR WORLD PEACE DAY, JANUARY 1, 2001, FROM THE VATICAN, DECEMBER 8, 2000

MANY PARTS, ONE BODY

For just as the body is one and has many members, and all the members of the body, though many, are one body, so it is with Christ. For in the one Spirit we were all baptized into one body—Jews or Greeks, slaves or free—and we were all made to drink of one Spirit.

Indeed, the body does not consist of one member but of many.... The eye cannot say to the hand, "I have no need of you," nor again the head to the feet, "I have no need of you." On the contrary, the members of the body that seem to be weaker are indispensable, and those members of the body that we think less honorable we clothe with greater honor, and our less respectable members are treated with greater respect....

1 CORINTHIANS 12:12–14, 21–23

PRAYER

Lord of all races and nations, there is too much division in the world. You took on human flesh for the sake of *all* people. Through your life and ministry, you bridged divisions and broke down barriers based on nationality, race, gender, physical capability, and social class. Help me recognize the value of people who are different from me. Teach me the wisdom of dialogue.

CHRISTMAS ACTION

Make a point to learn something from someone who is different from you or disagrees with you. Attend a multicultural event in the near future. If you a have a relationship that is suffering from a "cold war," make an effort to reopen the dialogue with that person.

DAY 12

The Missionary Call

*N*ow it is time to look to the future, and the story of the Wise Men can in a certain way give us our spiritual bearings. First of all, they tell us that when we encounter Christ, we must learn to stop and experience deeply the joy of intimacy with him. *"When they entered the house, they saw the child with Mary his mother, and bowing down they worshipped him"* [Matthew 2:11]: from now on their lives would be for ever given to the Child for whom they had endured the rigors of the journey and the deceitfulness of men. Christianity is born, and continually draws new life, from this contemplation of the glory of God shining on the face of Christ....

And yet, as in the case of the Wise Men, this immersion in contemplation of the mystery does not stop us from journeying on, indeed it compels us to start out afresh on a new stage of the journey on which we become proclaimers and heralds. *"They returned to their own country by a different way"* [Matthew 2:12].

The Wise Men were in a sense the first missionaries. Their encounter with Christ did not keep them in Bethlehem, but made them set out anew on the paths of the world. We need to set out anew from Christ and, in so doing, to set out anew from the Trinity.

JOHN PAUL II, HOMILY,
SOLEMNITY OF THE EPIPHANY, JANUARY 6, 2001

BRINGING THE GOOD NEWS TO OUR WORLD

Now the eleven disciples went to Galilee, to the mountain to which Jesus had directed them. When they saw him, they worshiped him; but some doubted. And Jesus came and said to them, "All authority in heaven and on earth has been given to me. Go therefore and make disciples of all nations, baptizing them in the name of the Father and of the Son and of the Holy Spirit, and teaching them to obey everything that I have commanded you. And remember, I am with you always, to the end of the age."

MATTHEW 28:16–20

PRAYER

Lord Jesus, God come into my world, this Christmas I met you as a baby in Bethlehem. While I would love to stay, gaze into your loving eyes, and merely contemplate the special gift of your presence with me, you have told me that I must go out into the world with the Good News I have received. Give me strength, courage, and wisdom as I take what I have learned and go forth with the message that our God is with us.

CHRISTMAS ACTION

How do you bring Christ to the world? Don't be afraid or ashamed to bear witness to Christ. Saint Francis is reported to have said, "Preach the gospel; use words when necessary." Make a point of sharing the Good News with someone today through word or deed. While, many people end their celebration of Christmas on December 25, remind someone of the good news of Jesus' birth by doing a small favor or giving a small gift (perhaps with religious significance) on this the twelfth day of Christmas.

PART III

~~~~~~~

A FORMAT for EVENING PRAYER

Format for Nightly Prayer and Reading

THE PURPOSE OF PRESENTING these two optional formats for nightly readings and prayer is to offer different ways to use the material in this book for group or individual prayer. Of course, there are other ways in which to use this book—for example, as a meditative daily reader or as a guide for a prayer journal—but the following familiar liturgical formats provide a structure that can be used in a variety of contexts.

FORMAT 1

OPENING PRAYER

The observance begins with these words:

> *God, come to my assistance.*
> *Lord, make haste to help me.*

followed by:

> *Glory to the Father, and to the Son,*
> *and to the Holy Spirit, as it was in the beginning,*
> *is now, and will be, for ever. Amen. Alleluia!*

EXAMINATION OF CONSCIENCE

If this observance is being prayed individually, an examination of conscience may be included. Here is a short examination of conscience; you may, of course, use your own preferred method.

1. Place yourself in a quiet frame of mind.
2. Review your life since your last confession.
3. Reflect on the Ten Commandments and any sins against these commandments.
4. Reflect on the words of the gospel, especially Jesus' commandment to love your neighbor as yourself.
5. Ask yourself these questions: How have I been unkind in thoughts, words, and actions? Am I refusing to forgive anyone? Do I despise any group or person? Am I a prisoner of fear, anxiety, worry, guilt, inferiority, or hatred of myself?

PENITENTIAL RITE (OPTIONAL)

If a group of people are praying in unison, a penitential rite from the Roman Missal may be used:

Presider: Lord Jesus, you came to call all people to yourself: Lord, have mercy.

All: Lord, have mercy.

Presider: Lord Jesus, you come to us in word and prayer: Christ, have mercy.

All: Christ, have mercy.

Presider: Lord Jesus, you will appear in glory with all your saints: Lord, have mercy.

All: Lord, have mercy.

Presider: May almighty God have mercy on us, forgive us our sins, and bring us to life everlasting.

All: Amen.

HYMN: "O COME, O COME, EMMANUEL"

A hymn is now sung or recited. This Advent hymn is a paraphrase of the great "O" Antiphons written in the twelfth century and translated by John Mason Neale in 1852.

O come, O come, Emmanuel,
And ransom captive Israel;
That mourns in lonely exile here,
Until the Son of God appear.

Refrain: Rejoice! Rejoice!
O Israel! To thee shall come, Emmanuel!

O come, thou wisdom, from on high,
And order all things far and nigh;
To us the path of knowledge show,
And teach us in her ways to go.

Refrain

O come, O come, thou Lord of might,
Who to thy tribes on Sinai's height
In ancient times did give the law,
In cloud, and majesty, and awe.

Refrain

O come, thou rod of Jesse's stem,
From ev'ry foe deliver them
That trust thy mighty power to save,
And give them vict'ry o'er the grave.

Refrain

O come, thou key of David, come,
And open wide our heav'nly home,
Make safe the way that leads on high,
That we no more have cause to sigh.

Refrain

O come, thou Dayspring from on high,
And cheer us by thy drawing nigh;
Disperse the gloomy clouds of night
And death's dark shadow put to flight.

Refrain

O come, Desire of nations, bind
In one the hearts of all mankind;
Bid every strife and quarrel cease
And fill the world with heaven's peace.

Refrain

PSALM 27:7–14—GOD STANDS BY US IN DANGERS

Hear, O LORD, when I cry aloud,
    be gracious to me and answer me!
"Come," my heart says, "seek his face!"
    Your face, LORD, do I seek.
    Do not hide your face from me.

Do not turn your servant away in anger,
    you who have been my help.
Do not cast me off, do not forsake me,
    O God of my salvation!
If my father and mother forsake me,
    the LORD will take me up.

Teach me your way, O LORD,
and lead me on a level path
because of my enemies.
Do not give me up to the will of my adversaries,
for false witnesses have risen against me,
and they are breathing out violence.

I believe that I shall see the goodness of the LORD
in the land of the living.
Wait for the LORD;
be strong, and let your heart take courage;
wait for the LORD!

RESPONSE

I long to see your face, O Lord. You are my light and my help. Do not turn away from me.

SCRIPTURE READING

Read silently or have a presider proclaim the Scripture of the day that is selected.

RESPONSE

Come and set us free, Lord God of power and might. Let your face shine on us and we will be saved.

Glory to the Father, and to the Son,
and to the Holy Spirit, as it was in the beginning,
is now, and will be for ever. Amen.

SECOND READING

Read the excerpt from Pope John Paul II for the day selected.

CANTICLE OF SIMEON

Lord, now you let your servant go in peace;
  your word has been fulfilled:
My own eyes have seen the salvation
  which you have prepared in the sight of every people:
A light to reveal you to the nations
  and the glory of your people Israel.
Glory to the Father, and to the Son, and to the Holy Spirit,
as it was in the beginning, is now, and will be for ever. Amen.

PRAYER

Say the prayer that follows the selected excerpt from Pope John Paul II.

BLESSING

May the Lord grant us a restful night and a peaceful death. Amen.

MARIAN ANTIPHON

Loving mother of the Redeemer,
  gate of heaven, star of the sea,
    assist your people who have fallen yet strive to rise again.
To the wonderment of nature you bore your Creator,
  yet remained a virgin after as before.
You who received Gabriel's joyful greeting,
  have pity on us poor sinners.

FORMAT 2

OPENING PRAYER

The observance begins with these words:

> *God, come to my assistance.*
> *Lord, make haste to help me.*

followed by:

> *Glory to the Father, and to the Son,*
> *and to the Holy Spirit, as it was in the beginning,*
> *is now, and will be, for ever. Amen. Alleluia!*

EXAMINATION OF CONSCIENCE

If this observance is being prayed individually, an examination of conscience may be included. Here is a short examination of conscience; you may, of course, use your own preferred method.

1. Place yourself in a quiet frame of mind.
2. Review your life since your last confession.
3. Reflect on the Ten Commandments and any sins against these commandments.
4. Reflect on the words of the gospel, especially Jesus' commandment to love your neighbor as yourself.
5. Ask yourself these questions: How have I been unkind in thoughts, words, and actions? Am I refusing to forgive anyone? Do I despise any group or person? Am I a prisoner of fear, anxiety, worry, guilt, inferiority, or hatred of myself?

PENITENTIAL RITE (OPTIONAL)

If a group of people are praying in unison, a penitential rite from the Roman Missal may be used:

All: I confess to almighty God,
and to you, my brothers and sisters,
that I have sinned through my own fault
in my thoughts and in my words,
in what I have done,
and in what I have failed to do;
and I ask blessed Mary, ever virgin,
all the angels and saints,
and you, my brothers and sisters,
to pray for me to the Lord our God.

Presider: May almighty God have mercy on us,
forgive us our sins,
and bring us to life everlasting.

All: Amen.

HYMN: "BEHOLD, A ROSE"

A hymn is now sung or recited. This traditional hymn was composed in German in the fifteenth century. It is sung to the melody of the familiar "Lo, How a Rose E're Blooming."

Behold, a rose of Judah
From tender branch has sprung,
From Jesse's lineage coming,
As men of old have sung.
It came a flower bright
Amid the cold of winter,
When half spent was the night.

Isaiah has foretold it
In words of promise sure,
And Mary's arms enfold it,
A virgin meek and pure.
Through God's eternal will
She bore for men a savior
At midnight calm and still.

PSALM 40:1–8—THANKSGIVING FOR DELIVERANCE

I waited patiently for the LORD;
    he inclined to me and heard my cry.
He drew me up from the desolate pit,
    out of the miry bog,
and set my feet upon a rock,
    making my steps secure.
He put a new song in my mouth,
    a song of praise to our God.
Many will see and fear,
    and put their trust in the LORD.

Happy are those who make
   the Lord their trust,
who do not turn to the proud,
   to those who go astray after false gods.
You have multiplied, O Lord, my God,
   your wondrous deeds and your thoughts toward us;
   none can compare with you.
Were I to proclaim and tell of them,
   they would be more than can be counted.

Sacrifice and offering you do not desire,
   but you have given me an open ear.
Burnt offering and sin offering
   you have not required.
Then I said, "Here I am;
   in the scroll of the book it is
      written of me.
I delight to do your will, O my God;
   your law is within my heart."

RESPONSE

May all who seek after you be glad in the Lord, may those who find your salvation say with continuous praise, "Great is the Lord!"

SCRIPTURE READING

Read silently or have a presider proclaim the Scripture of the day that is selected.

RESPONSE

Lord, you who were made obedient unto death, teach us to always do the Father's will, so that, sanctified by the holy obedience that joins us to your sacrifice, we can count on your immense love in times of sorrow.

Glory to the Father, and to the Son,
and to the Holy Spirit, as it was in the beginning,
is now, and will be, for ever. Amen.

SECOND READING

Read silently or have a presider read the words of Pope John Paul II for the day selected.

CANTICLE OF SIMEON

Lord, now you let your servant go in peace;
    your word has been fulfilled:
My own eyes have seen the salvation
    which you have prepared in the sight of every people:
A light to reveal you to the nations
    and the glory of your people Israel.
Glory to the Father, and to the Son, and to the Holy Spirit,
as it was in the beginning, is now, and will be for ever. Amen.

PRAYER

Recite the prayer that follows the excerpt from Pope John Paul II for the day selected.

BLESSING

Lord, give our bodies restful sleep and let the work we have done today bear fruit in eternal life. Watch over us as we rest in your peace. Amen.

MARIAN ANTIPHON

Hail, holy Queen, mother of mercy,
    our life, our sweetness, and our hope.
To you do we cry,
    poor banished children of Eve.
To you do we send up our sighs,
    mourning and weeping in this vale of tears.
Turn then, most gracious advocate,
    your eyes of mercy toward us,
    and after this exile
    show to us the blessed fruit of your womb, Jesus.
O clement, O loving,
O sweet Virgin Mary. Amen.